Turning

Green

By Barbara Rudow

CHAPTER ONE

GREEN'S THE NEW PINK

"Green is the new pink." That's a pretty catchy phrase, isn't it?

It means that caring about the environment is a growing trend. From movie stars to the family next door, it seems like everyone is "going green."

What does it mean to be green? Well, green is the color that stands for environmentalism (caring about the Earth). Living green means understanding that your actions have an effect on the environment. You try to live your life in a way that does as little damage as possible to the Earth. The simple choices all of us make every day are a big part of that.

Going green is a really important job: We have to save the world! Our planet is in great danger. Our air, our water, and our land are all threatened. And not only is the Earth at risk, but every one of us is also personally under attack. Many of the products we use and the foods we eat are harmful to us *and* the environment.

So, are *you* living green? There are a lot of questions you can ask yourself to help figure it out. Do you use products that are made with all-natural ingredients? Do you often ride in gas-guzzling cars? Do you eat organic foods? Do you recycle as much as possible? Do you leave lights on when you are not using them? Do you wear makeup that is harmful to the environment—and even your own face?

Most of us have mixed answers to these questions—some good, some bad. The trick is acting on your answers. You can make some simple, but possibly world-saving, changes in your own life. From morning until night, you make hundreds of choices that affect the environment. We all do. Together, if we make the right choices in being eco-friendly, we can make a big difference.

Former vice president Al Gore started talking about global warming a few years ago. At the time, many people didn't want to listen. (Global warming is a way of saying that our planet is heating up.) The title of Mr. Gore's documentary on global warming sums up the situation well: "An Inconvenient Truth."

Sure, it's easier to believe that there is no problem. Or that someone else will take care of it. But the *inconvenient* truth is that global warming, and other environmental issues, affect all of us. After all, there is only one planet Earth.

The reason that global warming is happening is because of a process known as the "greenhouse effect." This natural phenomenon gets its name from the way a greenhouse works. (A greenhouse is a glass building plants are grown in.)

Have you ever sat in a car with the windows rolled up on a sunny day? It gets hot pretty fast, right?

Well, that's how a greenhouse works, too. Heat from the sun passes through the glass. It warms up the ground inside the greenhouse (or the seats inside your car). This heats up the air above it. The warm air is trapped inside, keeping the greenhouse warm enough to grow plants all year long.

The greenhouse effect that's happening to our planet is a similar process. Certain gases in our atmosphere trap energy from the sun, called radiation. (These gases act like the glass in a greenhouse, and we call them greenhouse gases. They include carbon dioxide, methane, and nitrous oxide.)

This energy from the sun is what warms the Earth. So having *some* amount of these gases is actually good for the Earth's temperature. If these gases weren't there at all, the sun's radiation would bounce off the Earth. Then, the Earth would be too cold for us to live on. But now, we have way too much of these gases in our atmosphere.

Why? Well, over the last several hundred years, humans have begun to build things that produce these gases. Cars, airplanes, power plants, and factories all give off greenhouse gases.

And that's not all. There are also more of us humans now. That means more cars to drive us around and more factories to make all the stuff we need. So, those extra greenhouse gases are trapping a lot more of the sun's radiation. As a result, our planet is heating up: global warming.

Global warming affects more than just the temperatures around us. It can also change weather patterns. For example, warmer ocean water tends to produce bigger storms. (Think about the powerful hurricanes that have recently hit the United States, like Katrina, Rita, and Wilma.)

Our oceans are at the center of other scary climate trends as well. In recent years, as oceans have become warmer, water levels have risen. This may be because, as the water warms due to global warming, the ice near the North and South Poles begins to melt. This adds more water to the ocean. These deposits of ice, which are called the polar ice caps, are huge. When chunks of them start to melt and collapse into the ocean, they can quickly disappear. Think of an ice cube in a glass of water. It will melt a lot faster if there are fewer ice cubes around it.

In 2002, a giant chunk of ice (about 1,300 square miles in size) collapsed into the ocean. Some scientists fear that if warming continues, more of these giant chunks of ice will break off and melt into the ocean. If they do, many coastal areas around the world will be flooded. Millions of people living in coastal areas could lose their homes. Or worse—entire cities could be destroyed.

As the polar ice caps melt, polar bears like this one find it harder to survive. In fact, researchers were startled to find polar bears having to swim up to 60 miles across open sea to find food and a place to rest. Many are drowning or starving to death because of it.

Some of the side effects of rising temperatures are harder to see. That's because they are occurring *below* the surface of the ocean. Global warming is causing the destruction of thousands of miles of coral reefs, and we must protect them.

Coral reefs have often been called "tropical rainforests of the ocean." That's because of the great number of plant and animal species they support. Reefs protect our shorelines, and are a key part of our oceans' food chain. In one year (1998), 16 percent of the world's reefs were lost!

Can you imagine if we lose our reefs and beaches altogether? What would the side effects be on the rest of nature?

Despite the scary trends, there is some good news. We can help the coral reefs recover. We can stop the Earth from warming. We can help keep storms from growing stronger. We can take control of the chemicals we put into our bodies, our water, and our air. In other words, we can save our planet if we each do our part!

There is no simple fix. It took the whole world to get us into this mess. And it will take every one of us to get us out. We've spent the last few hundred years turning the world into a polluted mess. Now we have to spend the next few hundred turning it green again.

Millions of individuals have begun to do their part. Environmental groups have worked hard to spread the word. There are thousands of initiatives being put into effect by governments and organizations all over the world. They include recycling projects, clean-air acts, and many other small steps toward saving planet Earth.

The Kyoto Protocol was the first real effort to begin reducing the production of greenhouse gases on a *global* scale. Since 1997, 182 countries have agreed to the protocol. They have promised to monitor and reduce their own greenhouse gas emissions. (The United States has not yet agreed to the protocol.)

Celebrities have also become involved in the green movement. Leonardo DiCaprio is one of the celebrities leading the way. He produced the documentary "The 11th Hour." And he has also encouraged celebrities to skip the limousines at the Oscars and arrive in hybrid cars instead.

GREEN FACT: Hybrid cars use about half the gas regular cars do. Plus, they spit out 89 percent fewer harmful emissions. So when you drive a hybrid, fewer greenhouse gases are going into our atmosphere. Of course, when you walk or ride a bike, NO harmful chemicals are emitted!

Cameron Diaz and Chevy Chase were just two of the celebrities that joined in. Sheryl Crow went a step further. She actually toured the country in a bus that was powered by vegetable oil. Fuel made from vegetable oils is called "biodiesel." It can be made from leftover oil from fast food restaurants like McDonald's. Crow thought her eco-friendly bus was fun to ride in ... even though she said it smelled like french fries the entire way!

Other celebrities like George Clooney, Ed Norton, Robert Redford, Cate Blanchett, and Tom Hanks are going green, too. They do their part to raise money and awareness for the green movement.

Sure, these are small steps. But when you multiply these small steps several *billion* times, they really add up. To turn the world green again, millions and millions of non-politicians and non-celebrities will have to do their part as well.

In the following pages, you'll read about how young people can make a huge difference in saving the planet. For 17-year-old Jessica Assaf, becoming an active part of the green movement was personal and unexpected. After learning about some questionable practices in the makeup industry, she stood up for herself … and for planet Earth.

CHAPTER TWO

ONE PERSON MAKES A DIFFERENCE

Jessica Assaf started attending The Branson School, a high school in Northern California, in 2003. To graduate, each student has to complete a certain number of community service hours each year. Jessica was drawn to a local initiative known as "Teens for Safe Cosmetics."

Jessica had been wearing makeup since she was 13, so the topic was definitely interesting to her. Still, she was unsure about what the group was all about. She knew that makeup is used by millions of people every day. But she didn't understand how it could possibly be unsafe to people and the environment.

Didn't the companies who make the makeup

care about the health of the people who wore it? Didn't they feel responsible to keep the world free of pollutants? Wasn't *somebody* monitoring them to make sure their ingredients weren't bad for people and the environment? The more answers Jessica found to these questions, the more disturbed she became.

Like millions of other teenagers, Jessica started to wear lip gloss and nail polish at about the age of 12. She and her friends later started doing makeovers on each other. By high school, putting on makeup was part of their daily routines.

Toxic?

Jessica never thought about the harmful effects the chemicals used in producing makeup were having on the environment. And not once did she turn a box of makeup over to read the ingredients. Even if she had, they wouldn't have meant anything to her. The jumble of scientific names might as well have been written in a foreign language. To Jessica and most girls, makeup was pure fun. They didn't give it any thought beyond what they saw in the mirror.

That's why her first meeting with Judi Shils wasn't something she was taking too seriously. (Judi founded Teens for Safe Cosmetics.) Being a part of this group just sounded like a fun way to fill her graduation requirement. Jessica had no idea that this meeting would change her life.

The meeting took place at Branson High. Jessica and three other high school girls attended. Judi Shils and a chemist who had worked for several major cosmetics companies were also there. The chemist spoke to the group about the harmful ingredients in cosmetics. After he had spoken for about five minutes, the girls were totally floored.

They soon found out a scary fact: Many of the products they were using were harmful to them *and* the environment. The ingredients in the products included a long list of toxic chemicals. Some of these chemicals were linked to cancer, birth defects, reproductive disorders, and other health problems.

These poisonous chemicals were in the products they used every day—and nobody ever told them! To make matters worse, they were manufactured and disposed of with little regard for the environment. So even people who didn't wear makeup suffered.

Jessica was astonished. *Why didn't people know*

about this? she wondered. In an instant, Jessica went from being totally confused to totally upset. And then she went to the bathroom, where she washed all of the makeup from her face.

When she returned, the chemist began talking about a makeup company that he had once worked for. Jessica asked if he thought the owners of the company used their own products. The answer made her cringe. Not only did they not use them, he said, they thought they were junk.

The second thing that alarmed Jessica was when she found out that cosmetics are not regulated by the U.S. Food and Drug Administration (or FDA for short). The FDA is a government agency responsible for making sure our food and products are safe. They inspect, test, and set standards for products that are made and sold in the United States.

The FDA is largely responsible for food providers listing nutritional information. To be healthy, people need to know what they are putting into their bodies.

Cosmetics are not like most other products. They do *not* have to be approved by the FDA before they are sold. That means that companies can use any ingredients they want in their products. Even if they are harmful to people and the environment.

This information got Jessica so fired up that she decided to take immediate action. Jessica left the meeting with a list of harmful chemicals in hand. Then she went straight home to check the ingredients that were in *her* makeup products.

GREEN INFO: www.cosmeticsdatabase.com is a great website for checking the ingredients in your makeup and personal care products.

She quickly discovered that almost all of the products she used contained potentially harmful ingredients. Totally grossed out, Jessica grabbed all of her makeup and threw it away. This was a huge deal because Jessica loved makeup. And she had invested a lot of money in her collection of products. The truth was, she didn't want to stop wearing makeup altogether. Instead, she wanted to find products that both looked good and were safe to use. She saw no reason to risk her health over nail polish or mascara. Especially because she could get the same look from safer products!

What makeup *is* safe to use and not harmful to

the environment? That is one of the questions that Teens for Safe Cosmetics (also referred to as TSC) and the national Campaign for Safe Cosmetics are helping to answer.

The two groups work closely together and have similar goals. First, they want to educate the public about the potentially toxic ingredients in makeup and personal care products. Both groups also try to spread information about the existence of "green" alternatives (environmentally friendly versions).

The girls from TSC learn more about potentially toxic ingredients during a presentation.

After a short time, Jessica became very pas-sionate about TSC's cause. Still, she preferred to stay in her "comfort zone." This was on the sidelines and away from the spotlight. Jessica had always been very shy and didn't like to be the center of attention.

But her strong belief that people needed to know the truth about the products they were using changed all that. Through her experiences with TSC, Jessica became comfortable speaking in public. In fact, she eventually became the main spokesperson for TSC.

Jessica's public speaking career kicked off when she was a 14-year-old freshman. Although she was very nervous, she committed to doing a presentation in front of the entire school. She felt that she simply *had* to share her knowledge about environmentalism and safe cosmetics, in particular. Despite her enthusiasm, she was scared to death!

It's every teen's worst nightmare to do something embarrassing in front of the entire school. And of course, Jessica did just that. With the entire school watching her, Jessica carefully walked up the steps and onto the stage. Just as she hit the second to last step, she tripped. Then she fell to the ground, face first with a thud. Laughter rippled through the auditorium. In that moment, all she wanted to do was crawl away and hide. Instead, she stood up and bravely kept walking toward the podium. She took a deep breath and proceeded.

Jessica told the audience that they could each make a difference in saving the planet, and themselves. Her main point was this: Since everybody uses personal care products, this was a really simple place to start. "Toxic chemicals are not only harmful to our bodies—they are harmful to our environment. By taking some small steps to make ourselves healthier, we are also helping our planet," she said at the beginning of her speech. "It's a no-brainer."

She challenged her classmates to think about how the toxic chemicals in the products they use are made and disposed of. She handed out fliers with lists of dangerous chemicals they could look out for. "Do you really want to support companies that are polluting the Earth?" she asked. "Do you really want to put these disgusting toxins on your body?"

Look through *your* medicine cabinet today! (Many of the products you use may be toxic.) Then, check out the index of this book, to find a list of "greener alternatives." Why put harmful chemicals on your body?

Jessica's passion for her subject was clear. But she could tell that many of her classmates remained unconvinced. Some were interested in learning more. But others thought she was making too big of a deal out of something like makeup. Jessica was not about to give up, though.

"This issue is not just about changing lipstick and deodorant," she told them. "It's about social justice." She could tell that the audience was starting to get it. Jessica ended her speech by saying, "Putting poisonous chemicals in our makeup without telling us is a violation of our trust. As consumers, we expect that we are buying products that are safe. If that is not the case, don't we have a right to know?"

TSC believes that people *do* have a right to know. So they came up with a list of the most toxic chemicals in the makeup commonly used by teens. This list is known as the "Dirty Dozen +" (see index).

To create this list, TSC sent surveys to over 500 teens. They discovered that most of them used about 10 to 20 personal care products per day. They also found that many of the teenagers were using the same brands. They took the most popular items from that list. Then they researched the ingredients in each product (with the help of their chemist friends, of course).

The list they created made them sick. They found toxic chemicals in almost every product. There was some stuff that was just plain gross. For example, they found out that one of the ingredients in popular mascaras is also used to clean airplane wheels. Do you really want that stuff near your eyes?

Of course, people were not going to just stop using their favorite products. TSC had to let people know about alternatives to switch over to. So they came up with a list of "safe" companies. These are companies that use "green alternatives" to make great products. This list, titled "Greener Alternatives" (see index), was printed on the back of the flier for the Dirty Dozen.

Green makeup looks the same as regular makeup, although it tends to be lighter

The Dirty Dozen fliers were first handed out when "Operation Beauty Drop" was launched. Operation Beauty Drop was TSC's first "action." TSC decided to organize at least one action each month to spread the word about safe and unsafe products. For this event, they decorated drop-boxes and put them at places like malls and supermarkets. At these places, people could drop off their empty makeup and product containers. They also received a flier with the Dirty Dozen and Greener Alternatives lists.

GREEN INFO: These lists can be seen at **www.teensforsafecosmetics.org**. This website will also tell you more about Teens for Safe Cosmetics.

Operation Beauty Drop helped the team find out what products were being used. TSC could also educate the public about those products.

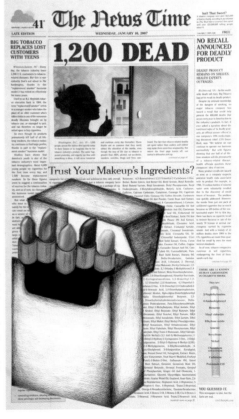

To get people to come by, the team created posters, flyers, and a giant face using the empty containers and the Dirty Dozen list. It was hard to miss, which was exactly what they wanted. But was it enough?

CHAPTER THREE

GREEN GLITZ AND GLAM

Teens love music, so TSC chose to have a "Battle of the Bands" as the entertainment for their next event. They wanted to get their message out to as many people as possible. Ten bands were selected to compete, and each band was asked to play one set. Local celebrities and teachers acted as judges. The first place winner would get the opportunity to use a recording studio for an entire day. This attracted a lot of up-and-coming bands to participate.

Hundreds of teens came, both to enjoy the music and to learn about green products. In between sets, Jessica and other members of TSC spoke about their campaign. Jessica was still a bit nervous speaking in public. But she was gaining confidence with each presentation.

Jessica was interviewed by a local radio station prior to a TSC event in 2007.

The Battle of the Bands was really successful. So when the next event was scheduled, music was incorporated again. This event was called the "Green Glitz and Glam Benefit Ball." It was held at Jessica's high school. About 350 people attended, which was a huge turnout! The event included a fashion show, dinner, and dance.

Jessica was extra-excited about this event because it reached beyond safe cosmetics. TSC wanted people to know you can "go green" in all areas of life, not just through personal care products. The girls talked about the environment, global warming, and green product alternatives. They also passed along simple steps that teens could take to change the world for the better.

A really cool part of this event was the runway they set up.

TSC searched for companies who were creating green fashion. All the fashions on the runway had to come from companies using only organic and sustainable products. They also had to be eco-friendly in their manufacturing. And they could not be involved in any unfair treatment of their workers. In other words, they wanted to find companies that stood for all the right things.

The words "organic" and "sustainability" are used a lot today. But what do they mean? The dictionary definition of sustainable is "capable of being continued with minimal long-term effect on the environment." Sustainable companies meet the needs of their company today. But they don't compromise the ability of future generations to meet their own needs.

Fortunately, there are many companies that have already "gone green." Clif Bar Inc. is a good example. The company uses recycled packaging, organic ingredients, and recycled paperboard for the containers that hold their nutrition bars. The recycled paperboard should save around 7,500 trees and 3.3 million gallons of water each year. How awesome is that? Think about how it would help our world if every company did that!

The word "organic" does not need to be scary. Organic clothing doesn't look any different than non-organic clothing. It is simply healthier for people and the environment. The difference is in how the item is grown and manufactured. Organic materials are grown without the use of chemicals. The manufacturing process also uses organic products and is eco-friendly.

Non-organic clothing starts out in fields covered in pesticides. These chemicals may stay in the material and eventually end up on your body. Think about this: A simple cotton T-shirt that is non-organic can take up to one-third of a pound of chemicals to make! Not only are consumers being exposed to those chemicals, but farm workers suffer, too. It is estimated that about 20,000 farm workers die every year in developing countries from pesticide poisoning. Many of these deaths come from cotton farming.

A lot of manufacturing processes use harmful chemicals (from chlorine to polyvinyl). And the toxic chemicals that you don't end up wearing often become waste that manufacturers have to get rid of. A lot of these chemicals eventually end up seeping into rivers, lakes, and even our drinking water. Gross!

Thirsty?

TSC wanted no part of that. At the fashion show, TSC proudly displayed all-organic clothing, makeup, and accessories—and they were amazing! Many of the featured fashions were provided by Stewart+Brown, a company that specializes in organic clothing. There were even prom dresses made using organic silk!

The food for the Green Glitz and Glam Benefit Ball was donated from some of the best restaurants in Northern California. The dinner included organic pasta, salad, and pizza.

GREEN FACT: Foods can only be labeled "organic" if they meet the standards set by the U.S. Department of Agriculture (USDA). If a product is labeled "organic," it means that a certified government worker inspected the farm where it was grown. He or she makes sure that the growers followed all the rules to meet the USDA organic standards. The farmers must use sustainable farming methods, meaning that they don't hurt the environment. This includes preserving agricultural land and treating animals fairly.

After the dinner, the Green Glitz and Glam Benefit Ball moved on to the fashion show. The models wore sustainable clothing for all occasions, from casual and formal attire to sleepwear. The models were all local teens, too—which was a cool touch.

Because the prom was only a few months away, the organic prom dresses were a huge hit. The jewelry (made from recycled materials) also received major attention. But Jessica thinks it was the green makeup the models wore that made the biggest splash.

Jessica and another TSC member, Heather, were the hosts for the evening. Other members of TSC were models and dressers backstage. Even Jessica's family got involved. Her two teenage brothers filmed the event. In the past, they had teased Jessica about her campaign. But now, they were starting to appreciate what their sister was trying to do.

By "turning green" with your clothing and products, you don't have to completely change your look. You only have to change some of your lifestyle choices. And you are making an important statement: "I care about what happens to the planet."

This is TSC's message. Sure, it started with cosmetics. But they don't want people to just change their lipstick and nail polish. They want people to make informed decisions about *all* products, from makeup to clothing to food.

Judi Shils, leader of TSC, says, "If people are mindful about what they put *on* their body, they'll be mindful about what they put *in* their body." Remember, turning green has no limits—you just keep on turning!

CHAPTER FOUR

SACRAMENTO, HERE WE COME

In 2005, TSC was contacted by California State Senator Carole Migden. She had heard about the work the group was doing. The senator was trying to pass a bill called the California Safe Cosmetics Act of 2005. Senator Migden thought the group might be able to help.

The California Safe Cosmetics Act, if passed into law, would require the makers of cosmetics and body-care products to do something new. They would have to start listing all the ingredients in their products—especially those linked to cancer, birth defects, or reproductive problems. The list would go to the California Department of Public Health and be available to all. This would be a big step in the fight for safer cosmetics. People could actually find out what was in the products they were using.

But taking on a billion-dollar industry was going to be tough. The cosmetics companies were fighting hard against the passage of this bill. They knew it was going to cost them extra money—and maybe even expose their unsafe practices to the public!

TSC agreed to help Senator Migden, and the girls quickly sprung into action. Jessica had never done anything like this before. She recalled history lessons about the state government. But she never dreamed that she would actually become involved.

The California State Legislature is made up of two houses: the Senate and the Assembly. There are 40 senators and 80 assembly members. Together, they represent the people of California.

Jessica knew that the passage of this bill would be very significant. After all, more than 35 million people live in sunny California. Beyond that, the passage of this bill would have a huge impact on every American who buys cosmetics.

The first step toward getting a bill passed is to have a senator or assembly member decide to "author" a bill. (This means that he or she is the person in charge of getting it passed). In this case, Senator Migden had already agreed to author the California Safe Cosmetics Act.

Carole Migden was the author, and a state senator. So her bill would first be presented to the Senate, then to the Assembly. The bill would be carefully reviewed before being put to a vote. If both houses passed the bill, it would be sent to the governor. He would then have three choices: sign it into law, allow it to become a law without his signature, or veto it. (A veto would mean that the bill is squashed.) On the other hand, if it is approved, it becomes part of the California Codes. These are a collection of laws used to govern the state.

When Senator Migden contacted TSC, the California Safe Cosmetics Act was about to be presented to the Senate. (The bill was also known as Senate Bill 484, or SB 484 for short.) She did not expect it to pass. But TSC was determined to give it a fighting chance.

The first thing TSC decided to do was go to Sacramento, California's state capital. Here they lobbied (voiced their support) for the bill. Judi Shils and five members of TSC carried signs declaring their cause. They spoke with anybody who would listen.

None of the TSC members had ever done anything like this before. So they wisely hired a lobbyist to show them the ropes. A lobbyist is a person who tries to influence public officials to take certain actions. In this case, it was to vote for the California Safe Cosmetics Act.

The lobbyist who helped them, Mr. Pete Price, was awesome. He taught them how the process worked and how to approach the politicians.

Their mission on this first visit was to explain what SB 484 was, and why it was so important. They were able to talk with several state legislators. But they knew they would have to contact many more to influence this bill. Before heading home, they scheduled future meetings with everyone they could.

Jessica and several members of TSC prepare for their meetings in Sacramento.

The group made a second trip to Sacramento the following week. They spent the entire day at the Capitol building in meetings. They were desperately trying to get people to understand the importance of this issue. The bill would be the first step in holding companies responsible for their products. Consumers would be given the ability to make safe choices. How could people decide what products were safe if they had no idea what was in them?

Jessica and her group discovered that in Europe, more than 1,100 chemical substances had been *banned* for use in cosmetics. In the United States, only nine of these substances had been banned! The other 1,091 were still being used. Examples are ingredients such as coal tar (used in shampoo) and petrolatum (used to make lipstick shine).

If all of the countries in Europe have banned these chemicals, how come we are still using them?

Why are harmful chemicals allowed here when they are considered too dangerous for people in Europe? Jessica asked that question to any senator who would listen.

What Jessica discovered was that most companies play by the rules they are given. Since they are not *required* by law to list their ingredients, they don't. Clearly, it was time to change the rules.

The members of TSC were only teenagers. But they quickly realized that they could actually make a difference! The fact that they were so young probably worked to their advantage. The politicians had to listen to adults all the time. So seeing a group of girls who were so passionate about their cause made them take notice.

TSC's hard work paid off: With their support, SB 484 passed in both the Senate and the Assembly!

Still, despite all their efforts, the bill was not expected to be signed into law by Governor Arnold Schwarzenegger. In fact, the cosmetics industry spent tons of money lobbying against this bill, to make sure it wouldn't be passed.

Their position on why the bill shouldn't be passed was simple: It was going to cost them more money for no reason, they said. Many of the companies insisted that the amount of chemicals in their products was too small to be dangerous. Listing them would only cause an unnecessary panic, they claimed.

But how could they know that for sure when

many chemists were saying the exact opposite? Was that a risk worth taking? Jessica didn't think so.

There is not yet absolute proof that these chemicals directly cause cancer and other health problems. But, there is also no proof that the combination of them is *not* dangerous. In fact, some recent studies suggest that the "cocktail" of chemicals we put into our bodies is actually very dangerous.

Scientist have a pretty good idea about which chemicals are safe and which are dangerous. But there is little known about the results of mixing chemicals together over a long period of time in "chemical cocktails."

You may or may not believe that these chemicals are unsafe. But shouldn't it be *your choice* what goes on your body, and not the cosmetics industry's choice?

This legislative process was both exciting and frustrating for Jessica. She was proud of what they were doing. But she sometimes felt as if they weren't making progress. The cosmetics industry had a lot more financial resources than TSC did.

Jessica was not about to give up, though—they had come too far. So, Jessica, Judi Shils, and several members of their team decided to make one last effort. They piled into the car and headed to Sacramento one more time. They were determined to meet with Governor Schwarzenegger himself.

When they got to the Capitol, they camped outside the governor's office. They held their signs high in the air. As Jessica says, they "spoke to anybody who looked important." They had been sitting for over two hours when they got some bad news. They were told that the governor was out of the

Governor Schwarzenegger

state. There was no way they could see him. It appeared as though they had traveled all this way only to be shot down. Jessica wanted to cry. Instead, she went into action.

The governor is a busy person, so every bill that comes before him is assigned to an analyst. The analyst does all the research regarding the issue. Then he or she makes a recommendation to the governor about whether the bill should pass. If TSC could speak with the analyst, they might still have a shot at getting the bill passed.

Jessica saw a man come out of the governor's office. She told him that she really needed to speak with the analyst assigned to the California Safe Cosmetics Act. The man told the girls he would see what he could do.

Outside on the bench, the nervous girls held hands. It all came down to this. To their surprise, their wish was granted: The man got them a meeting with the analyst assigned to SB 484! When the analyst let them into her office, she quickly said, "You each have five minutes."

The girls quickly scurried into the conference room.Jessica couldn't stop her hands from sweating. This was the state government, and she was only a 17-year-old. It was very intimidating!

Because of the short time limit, each girl tried to highlight different reasons why the bill should be passed. When it was her turn, Jessica pushed her fears aside. She began a passionate plea for every person's right to make informed decisions. Jessica argued that the companies should be required to list the ingredients. That way, people could decide for themselves which risks they did and didn't want to take.

Jessica went on to explain that most people use

10 to 20 personal care products on a daily basis. This means they are exposed to about 200 chemicals every day. Some of these chemicals may only be present in tiny (trace) amounts. But there is no conclusive research showing what the combinations of these chemicals do to our bodies with extended use.

Most people think that the products they use are regulated by the FDA. So they use them without thinking. The truth is that they aren't. Only 11 percent of 6,500 products on the market have been checked by the FDA. Listing the ingredients is a simple step that makes a lot of sense. And it is one that every person has the right to.

In the middle of Jessica's five minutes, the analyst started asking questions. The analyst was concerned about how much money the companies would lose if the bill passed. Instead of shying away from this question, Jessica argued that it wasn't important. After all, sacrificing a person's health for profit didn't make much sense, Jessica noted.

By the time they left, the girls from TSC still didn't know what would happen. The bill now sat on Governor Schwarzenegger's desk. And they couldn't be sure what he would do when he saw it.

They had done everything they could. Would their efforts be enough to pass the bill? They were hopeful, but couldn't be sure. They left the Capitol, gathering their signs for the long drive home.

CHAPTER FIVE

MAKEUP ARTISTS TO THE STARS

On October 7, 2005, the California Safe Cosmetics Act was signed into law by Governor Schwarzenegger. This was a huge victory for Jessica and TSC. They had taken on the cosmetics industry and won!

These teenagers (who were too young to even vote) fought hard for something they believed in. And they actually influenced the law and the world. You would think that would be enough, but not for Jessica. SB 484 was only the beginning.

In April 2007, TSC decided to do a "Don't Be Fooled" campaign. The project was designed to educate the public and to reach out to the companies themselves. To do that, they went to their Dirty Dozen list for help.

One professional who is studying the chemicals on the Dirty Dozen list is Dr. Maggie Louie, who got involved in studying this issue because of Jessica! She now lectures about toxic chemicals in makeup. She explains how the chemicals get absorbed into our bodies and stay in the fat tissue. Those chemicals can have a toxic effect over time—poisoning our bodies.

One particularly nasty family of chemicals is called phthalates. These chemicals are found in hair spray, nail polish, deodorant, gel, and other products. Phthalates have been associated with birth defects. They can cause damage to major body organs such as your kidneys, lungs, and liver. Talc, another harmful ingredient, is a main component in eye shadow, baby powder, and soap.

Check if the soap you use contains talc. If so, it may be toxic. A list of companies who sell "green" soap is available in the index.

Dr. Rebecca Sutton, a scientist at the Environmental Working Group, says, "We're not exposed to one chemical, our bodies absorb a soup of them every day. We don't know enough on how they affect our bodies when they interact, but we should be concerned."

GREEN INFO: Environmental Working Group (www.ewg.org) researches everything from protecting our air, to protecting your pet!

But people are not concerned enough. That's why TSC wanted to target the cosmetics companies themselves. Teens for Safe Cosmetics had nothing against these companies. In fact, they liked them. Remember, these girls joined TSC because most of them had an interest in makeup. They simply wanted to convince the companies to start turning green and produce healthier products.

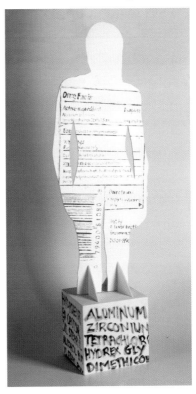

The first step in the "Don't Be Fooled" campaign was to make life-size wooden cutouts of some popular products. Their pri mary goal was to draw attention to the companies producing the products. If people knew the products contained harmful chemicals, they might stop using them. Then, the companies might offer green alternatives.

The second step was to hand out the Greener Alternatives lists. People would know which cosmetics companies truly put the health of their customers first. Unfortunately, their campaign didn't work as well as they had hoped. They got absolutely no response from the companies putting out the potentially harmful products.

Not willing to be ignored, some members of TSC teamed up with the national Campaign for Safe Cosmetics. They wanted to try a different approach. They decided to go to the professionals, and hosted an event for makeup artists in Los Angeles. Famous makeup artists were invited to come and try green makeup alternatives, provided by Iredale Mineral Cosmetics.

The chemicals in most makeup brands may be harmful to people who use just a small amount each day. Imagine what effect they could have on those who use them *all day long*. The thought behind TSC's newest project was simple: Let the makeup professionals know about the toxins in their favorite products. Then maybe they would help influence the companies to offer green alternatives.

Being a Hollywood makeup artist can be very

glamorous. Many of these makeup artists work on films and with celebrities. A good makeup artist can make someone look like an alien, a monster, or a vampire! Makeup can make an actor look older, younger, completely different, or just plain beautiful. Some makeup artists take their jobs to the extreme—creating prosthetic devices (like fake noses or ears.) It is such an involved art form that there is now an Academy Award presented for Best Makeup.

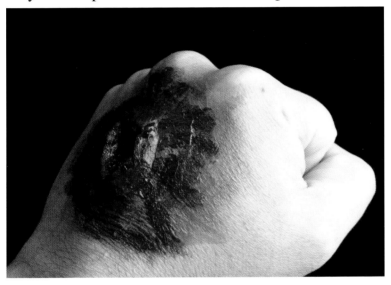

Don't worry, that's not a real gun shot wound...it's the handiwork of a talented makeup artist.

This may sound like pure fun, but are there dangers in this exciting job? Sadly, the answer is yes. These artists are exposed to an incredible number of chemicals. The hair spray, cosmetics, spray-on tans, dyes, and oils are only a few of the products they have to deal with. The makeup we put on our bodies is potentially harmful. Think about how it affects the makeup artists who handle hundreds of the products every day?

Jessica asked some of the makeup artists that very question. She was amazed by what she heard. She listened to story after story of health-related problems. These professionals believed they were caused by using unsafe products on a daily basis. Many of them spoke of reproductive problems, asthma, numbness, cancer, and everything in between.

Some of the makeup artists seemed open to trying green alternatives. But most were hesitant about changing their products. They are in an environment where the makeup they apply must stay on all day under difficult conditions. This requires very heavy makeup—and green makeup tends to be much lighter. This was a concern that many of the makeup artists voiced to Jessica.

There is some good news on the horizon, though. The popularity of high-definition television (HDTV) may change Hollywood's use of heavy makeup. That's because HDTV shows amazing detail, including wrinkles, pores, and other flaws.

To create the looks they want, actors must still use makeup. But if the makeup is too thick, it will show on HDTV. So, lighter makeup is starting to become more popular. Perhaps this is the opportunity green makeup companies have been waiting for! If even one makeup artist turns green, we will be one step closer to a healthier planet. After all, if movie stars begin using green makeup, millions of people will probably follow.

Many of the artists Jessica spoke with were excited about the green makeup they tried out that day. A few even vowed to stop using unsafe products.

The only way to truly change things, however, is for many people to demand change. If consumers continue to buy cosmetics from companies that use toxic chemicals, they are not giving these companies any reason to change. But if consumers refused to buy their products, those companies would have to consider changing. After all, for many cosmetics companies, it's all about the green—which is the color of money! If you don't give them any of your money, you will force them to turn *environmentally green.*

OPI is a good example of a major company that listened to its customers and made a change. OPI makes the most popular nail polish in the world. That is why the Campaign for Safe Cosmetics, along with TSC, decided to target that company.

OPI had already turned green in Europe, where they no longer use toxic chemicals. This meant that the company already had the formula to eliminate toxins from their U.S. brand. The trick was getting them to see that Americans (like Europeans) thought healthy and environmentally safe products were important.

Jessica had a personal interest in this because OPI used to be her favorite product. She really missed using it. She wanted OPI to get rid of the toxic chemicals in their nail polish. Until then, she would not support the company or use their products.

TSC wanted OPI to use the same green practices they use in Europe here in the United States. So TSC members went to the streets to educate consumers and raise awareness of their cause. They hung out all day at the trendy Third Street Promenade in Santa Monica, California.

The Santa Monica Pier.

The girls wanted to be sure they were noticed, so they dressed up as beauty queens. Their outfits had sashes that said "Miss Treatment." This play on words highlighted how they believed OPI was treating its customers (or mistreating them). When they were not talking to people, the girls marched together and sang the chant they wrote: *1-2-3-4 ... Toxic chemicals no more.5-6-7-8 ... OPI reformulate!*

The media were there to capture the event, so Jessica used the opportunity to reach even more people. She spoke in front of the news cameras and asked people to call OPI. She wanted them to tell OPI that they would not use their products until they stopped using poisonous ingredients. It turns out that many people did make that call!

Shortly after the rally, a *Los Angeles Times* reporter called OPI for a statement. With all the pressure from their customers, OPI said that they *did* plan to change their formula! They were removing dibutyl phthalate (DBP), the toxic chemical Jessica had asked them to remove, from all of their products. The team at TSC had done it again!

CHAPTER SIX

THE BROWER AWARDS

In April 2006, Jessica got a phone call that changed her life. She was told that she had won a Brower Youth Award! This important award is like the Oscars for young environmental activists. Jessica was honored just to be considered for the award. So when she got the call that she had won, she was stunned.

Each year, the Brower Youth Award is presented to six people from ages 13 to 22. They are selected from all over North America. Brower Youth Award recipients are considered to be the leading environmental advocates in the country.

The award is named after David Brower, an environmentalist who spent his life working for conservation. David loved mountain climbing and the wilderness. That love led him to become the first executive director of the Sierra Club, America's oldest and largest environmental organization. Mr. Brower was also the founder of the Earth Island Institute. This organization is dedicated to promoting projects and leaders committed to the protection of our environment. The Earth Island Institute is the organization behind the Brower Youth Awards.

At first, Jessica was reluctant to apply for the award. Judi Shils had nominated her a few months back, though. So she felt like she owed it to her to follow through. Jessica believed strongly in what she was doing, but she was sure that others were doing bigger things.

Luckily, Judi persuaded her to go for it. This 17-year-old had already influenced major companies. She'd helped to get a Senate bill passed, and educated countless people on their right to make safe and healthy choices. Jessica was still actively working on these projects. By receiving this award, she

Jessica and Judi Shils at the Brower Awards ceremony.

would be in a position to do even more.

The award ceremony was held in the historic Herbst Theatre in San Francisco. Jessica got there early. She got to see many of the current Earth Island projects, and visit with other winners while enjoying the hip-hop entertainment. There was plenty of food there, too (all organic of course!).

After the opening reception, Jessica nervously headed to her seat. Although she now spoke in public quite a bit, this night was different. The thought of standing up in front of hundreds of people who were waiting to honor her was overwhelming. Jessica felt like her heart was going to jump right out of her chest.

Jessica listened as the winners were announced. It was very impressive. The award recipients were introduced by showing a film about each recipient.

Prior to the ceremony, a film crew from Earth Island had gone to Jessica's hometown to film her story. They even followed Jessica to L.A. for the OPI rally.

GREEN INFO: To see Jessica's video and learn more about the Brower Youth Awards, visit **www.broweryouthawards.org**.

In addition to being recognized, the winners receive a cash award of $3,000 to help them continue their work. More importantly, they each gain access to all the resources at Earth Island Institute. The organization will help them promote their projects through research materials, publicity, and personnel. Jessica now had access to an entire environmental network!

The winners were also treated to a week of fun. They traveled together in a biodiesel bus and spoke about their projects at a number of high schools. The winners also got to go on a camping trip to Point Reyes National Park in Northern California.

Prior to this, Jessica's idea of camping was a hotel. Her idea of hiking was walking around the mall. On her camping trip, Jessica discovered that in addition to *saving* the environment, she really enjoyed hanging out there. Jessica hiked, swam, and even ate her first s'more!

Being away from home gave Jessica a chance to bond with the other recipients. Friendships were formed that would last long after their road trip ended.

Although Jessica has many friends at school, she sometimes feels like she is a little different. Her passion is working with TSC, not playing sports or attending high school activities. This often makes her feel as if there is no one with whom she truly connects. All of that changed after she received the Brower Youth Award. Suddenly, Jessica found herself surrounded by teens who shared her passion for protecting our planet.

CHAPTER SEVEN

PROJECT PROM

There was one school activity that Jessica *was* excited about: the prom. Jessica wanted to use the excitement of the prom as the theme for TSC's next event. Obviously, most girls wear makeup to the prom. So showing teens how great the green alternatives could be was a natural fit.

On the day of their prom, many girls go to department stores to get makeovers. TSC decided to offer their own makeovers using only green products. This would be a great way for girls to try the makeup.

Jessica was interviewed by a local newspaper before the event. She said, "Teens should be able to look their best at prom without worrying about the burden of all those chemicals."

The event grew bigger and bigger in the days leading up to the prom. In response to this, TSC decided to rent space in Union Square. Union Square sits in the middle of seven major department stores in San Francisco. These were the same stores where many girls would have their makeup done for prom.

TSC put up three tents in Union Square, each for a different purpose. One tent was for general information where they passed out the Dirty Dozen and Greener Alternatives fliers. A second tent, hosted by Whole Foods Market, offered mini-facials, as well as a sampling of organic products. In the third tent, professional skin care specialists provided free makeovers using all green products.

There was also a big stage where a full program took place. The Bob Hill Band (winner of the earlier TSC event, Battle of the Bands) played to help draw people into the area. The girls set up chairs so people could comfortably enjoy the music—and listen to some distinguished speakers. One of these speakers was Senator Migden. She spoke to the crowd about the importance of knowing what chemicals are in personal care products.

Jessica, in pink, above and below, addresses the crowd at Union Square in San Francisco.

The speakers, the tents, and the band drew a lot of attention. But that was nothing compared to the girls themselves. They came to the rally dressed in prom dresses, tiaras, and combat boots! (The boots represented their fight against toxic chemicals.)

There were about 30 campaign members dressed like that, so they drew quite a crowd wherever they went. One of their main goals in selecting the location near the department stores was to educate the makeup artists who worked there. They hoped that many of these makeup artists would drop by and try out some of the green products. TSC knew that if the public demanded safer products, the companies would change. That demand could get a kick start from the makeup pros.

Unfortunately, safe cosmetics can be hard to find in many places. They can also be expensive. Over time, with more people requesting them, they will become more available and affordable.

The 30 TSC crusaders, armed with signs and information, marched into the stores to spread their message. Jessica led the group as they wove single-file through the aisles of the first store. They looked like a giant, colorful snake. It was designed to be a peaceful rally, so the girls were pretty quiet. All they did was hand letters to the workers, which asked them to please offer at least one organic alternative.

It was all going great until Jessica looked up and saw a manager heading her way. He was talking into a walkie-talkie and did not look happy. The girls really stood out (which was exactly what they had intended). But that was apparently bad for business. So, the girls were kicked out of the store!

This was a first for most of the girls, and it was very disturbing. Jessica had never been in trouble before. To have people tell her she wasn't welcome was very upsetting. However, that did not discourage her from leading the girls to six other stores. Some of the stores welcomed them, but several of them asked the girls to leave. When they had been to all the major stores, they marched back outside. Jessica led the girls in a chant: *1 – 2 – 3 – 4 ... Toxic chemicals no more! 5 – 6 – 7 – 8 ... FDA must regulate!*

The day ended up being a huge success. The message was heard by many people. Since that rally, Barneys New York and Macy's have included green products in both their cosmetics and clothing departments! Many other stores are following this growing trend. It all starts with people willing to stand up for what is right. Once again, a few young girls helped to create big change. They also created some unplanned entertainment that day.

A very strange and random thing happened just as the rally was winding down. TSC member Erin Schrode thought that the most demanding thing she would be doing at the rally was carrying a sign and speaking to the crowd. However, after hearing the music at the rally stop, she looked over and saw three young men. They were running off with the laptop that had been powering the sound.

"I wasn't going to let them get away," Erin says. "Something in me just said: 'You're going to catch them.'" With that thought in mind, she started running after the boys. You can only imagine the looks on the faces of the crowd. Erin—dressed in a prom dress, combat boots, and a tiara—was running after the thieves through the city streets!

The race lasted several blocks. The crazy scene was like something out of a movie. People were cheering Erin on as she dodged cars and raced through the heart of San Francisco. As she ran, Erin yelled for people to stop the thieves. But in the end, it was Erin who caught one of them.

The police quickly arrived to help, and Erin was able to lead them to the second suspect. Unfortunately, they did not recover the laptop, but they did find a stolen purse and some cash. Erin's speed and bravery saved the day. The headline in a local paper read— **FASHION POLICE: Marin teen chases down thieves in S.F. while clad in prom dress, combat boots.**

After that incident, Erin was asked to be on The Tonight Show with Jay Leno and the national Fox News Channel! It was a bizarre ending to the otherwise peaceful—and successful—rally.

CHAPTER EIGHT

A BRIGHT GREEN FUTURE

Teens for Safe Cosmetics continues to grow and organize activities each month. Their first priority is makeup. But they hope that someday soon *all* companies will use safer ingredients in *all* products.

In the meantime, TSC is taking matters into their own hands. Jessica and several other campaign members recently worked with one of their partner companies (EO) to make their own line of perfume. The girls were given a variety of oils, which they mixed in different ways to create a scent that they thought teens would like. They created a fragrance that they all loved.

This perfume, called "I," is sold in sustainable packaging, so it is as green as it can be. TSC sells the perfume at their events, and the money is used to support their campaign. This has turned into a partnership with Whole Foods Market called "Teens Turning Green." They are hoping to launch a complete line of green products for teens by the fall of 2009.

Jessica has enjoyed every aspect of working with TSC. Although she hopes to continue to be involved, she is also ready to step outside her comfort zone yet again. Jessica once thought that after high school, she would stay close to home and attend a local college. But now, Jessica feels the need to go a bit farther and to explore the world from another view. Jessica's new path may take her as far as our nation's capital, Washington, D.C.

Jessica plans to study law, with the hope of working in public health. With her passion to make the world a safer place, this path would allow her to have a big impact. Her experiences have made her see that sometimes changing the law is the best way to get people to do what's right.

A good example of this is solar heating. Everyone agrees that solar heat can save both energy and money. Still, how many people have actually switched over to it? Well, Hawaii lawmakers, like Jessica, realize that people often need help to do what is right. Hawaii recently became the first state to pass a law requiring new homes to have a solar water heater.

The solar panels in the picture above help convert the suns rays into energy we can use.

Hawaii is taking a step toward turning green. And remember, that's all it takes—one step at a time. Think of the energy we'd save if every state did the same thing!

No matter where Jessica decides to go to college, one thing is for sure: We have not heard the last of her. Jessica says, "I want people to know that we must start now to sustain the world for future generations. We have all the resources and technology; all we need is for people to begin using environmentally safe products and practices."

When Jessica is asked why she got involved in Teens for Safe Cosmetics, she says: "It was an easy place for me to start. Using safer makeup affects you on such a personal level. I could go home and immediately make a difference." You can make a difference, too.

GREEN TIPS: For starters, recycle everything you can. It is estimated that 85 percent of what we throw away can be reused. Did you know that it takes 20 times more energy to make aluminum cans from scratch than from recycled ones? Think about the energy you could save the next time you toss your can in the trash.

Turn out the lights! When you leave a room, make sure everything is off. If you need to use lights, be sure they are compact fluorescent bulbs. Ask your parents what type of light bulbs are used in your house. Compact fluorescent bulbs use about 65 percent less energy than regular ones. (And they provide the same light at about the same cost.)

The environmentally friendly companct fluorescent bulb. Replace all your old light bulbs with these "green" bulbs!

You can also conserve water by taking shorter showers and making sure the faucets are completely turned off.

You can help reduce pollution by riding your bike more often, too. Cars contribute more than one-third of all the greenhouse gas emissions we produce! So when you can buy a car, buy a hybrid. Gas-guzzling SUVs can produce as much as 95,000 pounds of global-warming pollution in just one year!

Using safe makeup and personal care products should also be at the top of your list. It's up to you to take care of yourself, and to do your part in taking care of our planet. Organic products help both you and the environment. Every time you use organic products, you are taking one more step toward improving your world.

There are many more things that you can do. If you visit www.ecologue.com, you can find countless ways to get involved in the fight to save planet Earth. What you do matters. Jessica has shown us that teens *can* make a difference.

When the California Safe Cosmetics Act passed, Jessica discovered that she could truly affect the world. She says, "Seeing the law passed was very fulfilling. I learned that I can make a difference. All it takes is confidence and belief in the cause. I never believed that teenagers could have such an impact. But now I see that age is just a number, and teens have as much power to create change as adults. Sometimes, maybe more. ... We are the future, and we have all the tools for improvement. Everyone has the power to make change."

Jessica Assaf acted on those words, and you can, too! In fact, you *must*. Our planet is at risk, and it is up to all of us to make our future happy and healthy. Living green is not just a new fad, but a new way of life. And it all starts with you.

So how are you going to help turn the world green again?

The Dirty Dozen +
(Source: Teens for Safe Cosmetics)

The following is a list of potentially harmful chemicals to look for in your personal care products. If you see these chemicals, beware!

Butyl Acetate

Butylated Hydroxytoluene

Coal Tar

Cocamide DEA/Lauramide DEA

Diazolidinyl Urea

Ethyl Acetate

Formaldehyde

Parabens (methyl, ethyl, propyl and butyl)

Petrolatum

Phthalates

Propylene Glycol

Sodium Laureth/Sodium Laurel Sulfate

Talc

Toluene

Triethanolamine

GREENER ALTERNATIVES
(Source: Teens for Safe Cosmetics)

This is a list of companies making safer products. Check their websites and in your community, check out Whole Foods Market, Pharmaca, Good Earth, Elephant Pharmacy, and all of the local businesses who stock healthy alternatives.

ALAFFIA - alaffia.com, Hair, skin, lip and body care, soap

ASTARA - astaraskincare.com, Skin and body care. AURA CACIA - auracacia.com, Body care, bath, essential oils, perfume

BENEDETTA - benedetta.com, Skin and body care, soap, deodorant, hand sanitizer

BURT'S BEES - burtsbees.com, Hair, skin, lip and body care, soap, deodorant, makeup, sunscreen, insect repellent

CORAL WHITE - coral-cure.com/coral-white-toothpaste.htm, Toothpaste, mouthwash

DR. BRONNER'S - drbronner.com, Body and lip care, soap

DR. HAUSCHKA - drhauschka.com, Hair, skin, lip and body care, deodorant, makeup, sunscreen

DROPWISE ESSENTIALS - dropwise.com, Body and lip care

EARTHBOUND ORGANICS - www.earthbound.co.uk, Skin and body care, soap

ECO LANI - ecolani.com, Sunscreen

EDEN'S KISS - edenskiss.com, Body care, bath, anti-aging products

EO PRODUCTS - eoproducts.com, Hair, skin, lip and body care, bath, essential oils, hand sanitizer

EVAN HEALY - evanhealy.com, Skin and body care

GRATEFUL BODY - gratefulbody.com, Skin and body care

GREEN PEOPLE - greenpeople.com, Hair, skin, lip, and body care, deodorant, toothpaste, sunscreen

HERBAN COWBOY - herbancowboy.com, Shaving cream, soap, deodorant

HONEYBEE GARDENS - honeybeegardens.com, Lip and nail care, makeup

IREDALE MINERAL COSMETICS - janeiredale.com, Makeup

JA NENE - anointyourself.com, Skin and lip care, bath

JASON - jason-natural.com, Hair, skin, and body care, deodorant, toothpaste, sunscreen, soap

JOSIE MARAN - josiemarancosmetics.com, Makeup

JOHN MASTERS ORGANICS - johnmasters.com, Hair, skin, lip and body care, soap

JP DURGA - jpdurga.com, Hair, skin, lip and body care, soap

JUICE BEAUTY - juicebeauty.com, Skin and lip care

JURLIQUE - jurlique.com, Skin, lip and body care, soap, bath, makeup remover

KEYS - keys-soap.com, Skin, body and hair care, insect repellent, sunscreen

LAFE'S - lafes.com, Deodorant, foot spray

LOGONA - logona.co.uk, Hair, skin and body care, toothpaste, makeup

LAVERA - lavera.com, Hair, skin, lip and body care, makeup

MIESSENCE - miessenceproducts.com, Hair, skin and body care, makeup

MOOM - imoom.com, Body care

MYCHELLE - mychelleusa.com, Skin, lip and body care

NATRACARE - natracare.com, Feminine hygiene, organic cotton wipes

NUDE SKINCARE - nudeskincare.com, Makeup

ORGANIC APOTEKE - organicapoteke.com, Skin and body care, soap, perfume

PANGEA ORGANICS - pangeaorganics.com, Skin and body care, soap

PHARMACOPIA - pharmacopia.net, Body and lip care

POMEGA5 - pomega5.com, Skin and body care

RIVER SOAP - riversoap.com, Soap and bath

SIMPLY ORGANIC - simplyorganicbeauty.com, Hair, skin and body care

SPIRIT OF BEAUTY -nutritionskincare.com, Skin and lip care

SUKI - sukipure.com, Hair, skin, lip and body care, makeup

TWEEN BEAUTY - tweenbeauty.com, Hair and lip care

WELEDA - usa.weleda.com, Hair, skin and body care, toothpaste

ZUZU - gabrielcosmeticsinc.com, Makeup